ON THE CAMPAIGN TRAIL

HISTORY'S MOST INTERESTING CANDIDATES

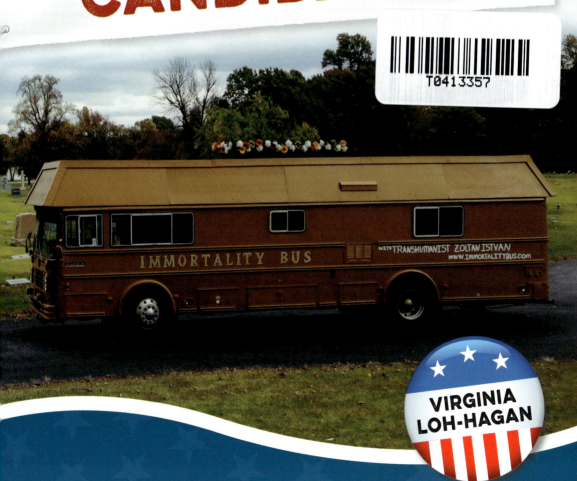

VIRGINIA LOH-HAGAN

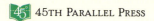
45TH PARALLEL PRESS

Published in the United States of America by Cherry Lake Publishing Group
Ann Arbor, Michigan
www.cherrylakepublishing.com

Reading Adviser: Beth Walker Gambro, MS, Ed., Reading Consultant, Yorkville, IL
Content Adviser: Mark Richards, Ph.D., Professor, Dept. of Political Science, Grand Valley State University, Allendale, MI
Book Designer: Frame25 Productions

Photo Credits: Zoltan Istvan Gyurko, CC BY-SA 4.0 via Wikimedia Commons, cover, title page; © Felix Mizioznikov/Shutterstock, 5; © Lost_in_the_Midwest/Shutterstock, 7; © Bill Chizek/Shutterstock, 9; © Madcat_Madlove/Shutterstock, 13; Marc Nozell from Merrimack, New Hampshire, USA, CC BY 2.0 via Wikimedia Commons, 17; © Gorodenkoff/Shutterstock, 19; © MadisonRae/Shutterstock, 23; Michael Foertsch, CC BY 4.0 via Wikimedia Commons, 27; © StunningArt/Shutterstock, 29; © CGN089/Shutterstock, 31

Copyright © 2025 by Cherry Lake Publishing Group

All rights reserved. No part of this book may be reproduced or utilized in any form or by any means without written permission from the publisher.

45th Parallel Press is an imprint of Cherry Lake Publishing Group.

Library of Congress Cataloging-in-Publication Data has been filed and is available at catalog.loc.gov

Cherry Lake Publishing Group would like to acknowledge the work of the Partnership for 21st Century Learning, a Network of Battelle for Kids. Please visit Battelle for Kids online for more information.

Note from publisher: Websites change regularly, and their future contents are outside of our control. Supervise children when conducting any recommended online searches for extended learning opportunities.

Printed in the United States of America

ABOUT THE AUTHOR

Dr. Virginia Loh-Hagan is an author and educator. She is currently the Director of the Asian Pacific Islander Desi American (APIDA) Center at San Diego State University and the Co-Executive Director of The Asian American Education Project. She lives in San Diego with her very tall husband and very naughty dogs.

CONTENTS

Introduction 4

Chapter 1: **Boston Curtis (1938)** 8

Chapter 2: **Pigasus (1968)** 10

Chapter 3: **Mr. Potato Head (1985)** 12

Chapter 4: **Vermin Love Supreme (1987)** 14

Chapter 5: **Keith Russell Judd (1996)** 16

Chapter 6: **Clay Henry III (2000)** 18

Chapter 7: **Raphael Klapper (2010)** 20

Chapter 8: **Mae Poulet (2012)** 22

Chapter 9: **Andrew Basiago (2016)** 24

Chapter 10: **Zoltan Istvan (2016)** 26

Do Your Part! 28

Glossary, Learn More, Index 32

INTRODUCTION

The United States is a top world power. It's not ruled by kings or queens. It's a **democracy**. A democracy is a system of government. It means "rule by the people." People **elect** their leaders. They choose leaders by voting.

Leaders **represent** the people who voted for them. They speak for them. They make decisions for them. That's why voting is so important. By voting, we choose our leaders.

Candidates run for **public office**. Public office is a government position. Candidates work hard to get votes. They run **campaigns**. They do this before an election. Campaigns are planned activities. Some campaigns are easy. Some are hard. And some are full of drama.

People line up to vote for their elected officials. It's a right and a privilege for U.S. citizens.

The U.S. government has many public offices. Each office has different rules. The U.S. president has the most rules. Only U.S. citizens can be president. Candidates must be at least 35 years old.

All states have elections. In most states, candidates must be at least 18 years old. They also must live in the state. However, some candidates find **loopholes**. Loopholes are unclear rules. They give people legal ways to go around the law.

U.S. history has many interesting candidates. Some have been animals. Some have been objects. This book features some of the fun ones!

Sometimes people find ways to work around the rules to nominate interesting candidates.

CHAPTER ONE
BOSTON CURTIS
(1938)

Kenneth Simmons (1904–1981) was the mayor of Milton. This town is in the state of Washington. Simmons was a joker. He had a brown mule. The mule's name was Boston Curtis. In 1938, Simmons took his mule to the courthouse. He put the mule on the **ballot**. Ballots are the voting ticket. They list all the candidates. The mule's hoofprint is on official records. It looks like a smeared mark.

Simmons signed up the mule for **precinct captain**. Precinct captains connect political parties and voters. The mule ran unopposed. People voted for it. They didn't know it was a mule. The mule won. It got 51 votes.

Simmons had a point. He said people vote without really knowing the candidates.

A mule is a cross between a horse and a donkey.

CHAPTER TWO

PIGASUS
(1968)

Pigasus was a pig. He weighed 145 pounds (65.8 kilograms). In 1968, he was nominated for U.S. president. It happened at the national convention of the Democratic Party. This took place in Chicago, Illinois.

The Youth International Party (YIP) was a political party. They were called Yippies. They believed in free speech. They opposed government. They liked to perform.

They hosted a rally. Seven Yippies escorted the pig in a big car. They announced Pigasus as a candidate. They said, "If we can't have him in the White House, we can have him for breakfast." They carried signs. They passed out posters. They caused a scene.

WORLD AFFAIRS

U.S. leaders must attend to world affairs. We're connected to what happens around the world. Other countries have interesting candidates, too. Ecuador is in South America. Picoazà is a small town there. About 19,000 people live there. It has a rich history. It has city remains from before the 1500s. Today, it's known for a strange election legend. People say in 1967, Pulvapies won the most votes for mayor. Pulvapies is a foot powder. Foot powder protects feet. It keeps them dry. It keeps them smelling fresh. It keeps them from itching. People say the Pulvapies company ran ads. They promoted the powder. They said, "Vote for any candidate. But if you want well-being and hygiene, vote for Pulvapies." Hygiene means health. It's said that the campaign worked. Pulvapies won the election.

CHAPTER THREE
MR. POTATO HEAD
(1985)

Mr. Potato Head is a toy. It's made of plastic. It's shaped like a potato. Plastic parts are added to it. These parts include ears, eyes, nose, and mouth. They make a face. Mr. Potato Head was the first toy advertised on TV.

Boise is in Idaho. Idaho is known for potatoes. In 1985, Mr. Potato Head ran for mayor. Its **slogan** was "A man of the soil." Slogans are catchy phrases.

Mr. Potato Head got 4 votes. It lost the election. But it got a world record for the "most votes for a toy in a political campaign." Mr. Potato Head's candidacy was a joke. Students from Boise State and the toy company did it.

THE IDEAL CANDIDATE

Ideal candidates are role models. In 1997, Stubbs the cat was found in a box. He was left in a parking lot of a store. Lauri Stec managed the store. She adopted Stubbs. Stubbs didn't have a tail. Stubbs was a true leader. He was the honorary mayor of Talkeetna in Alaska. It's a historic town. It doesn't have a government. It isn't well-known. But Stubbs made it famous. Tourists came to see him. Fans wrote him letters. They sent him cards. Stubbs built community. He was loved by all humans. But he did have an enemy. A dog attacked him. People donated money. They paid for his vet bills. Any extra money was given to rescue groups. The townspeople voted for him in the 2014 U.S. Senate race. Stubbs lost. But Stubbs served more than 20 years as mayor. He died in 2017. His owners said, "He was a trooper until the end of his life."

CHAPTER FOUR

VERMIN LOVE SUPREME
(1987)

Vermin Love Supreme (born 1961) loves running for office. His first campaign was for mayor of Baltimore, Maryland. He did that in 1987. Since then, he's run in state and local elections. He's run for president since 1992.

Supreme wears many ties. He wears a boot as a hat. He carries a large toothbrush. He gives interviews. He crashes events. He throws glitter.

If elected, he said he'd do many interesting things. He'd pass a law requiring people to brush their teeth. He'd use zombies as energy. He'd research time travel. He'd give each citizen a free pony.

Supreme runs as a joke. He's mocking the system. He said, "Together, we will ride our ponies into a zombie-powered future."

Vermin Love Supreme "glitter-bombed" another speaker at an event. It was the Lesser-Known Presidential Candidates Forum at St. Anselm's College.

CHAPTER FIVE

KEITH RUSSELL JUDD
(1996)

Keith Russell Judd (born 1958) has run for president since 1996. His nickname is the "Dark Priest." In 2012, he ran against President Barack Obama (born 1961). This was in the Democratic Party primaries. In West Virginia, he got 41 percent of the vote against Obama. He's also run for mayor and governor. He did this in New Mexico.

Judd is an unusual candidate. He was a **convict**. Convicts are guilty of a crime. Judd was sent to jail in 1999. He was sentenced to 17.5 years. His crime was sending threats over the mail. He mailed postcards. He sent knives. He tried to **extort** money from people. Extort means to unfairly take something.

Convicts can't vote. But they can run for president.

CHAPTER SIX
CLAY HENRY III
(2000)

Lajitas is in west Texas. About 100 people live there. It's a small town. It's not well-known. But its mayor is famous. Clay Henry was known as a "beer-drinking goat."

Clay Henry became popular. He was elected mayor in 1986. Since then, his kids have been elected mayor.

In 2000, the town's ballot was interesting. It included the 3rd goat Clay Henry of the town. It included a wooden statue. It included a dog. It even included a person. But he was not well-liked. He was from Houston. Houston is another city in Texas. Locals wanted a mayor from the town. Clay Henry III was local. He was born and raised in Lajitas. He won the election.

Tourists can still visit Lajitas to see the original Clay Henry. But he's stuffed now.

CHAPTER SEVEN
RAPHAEL KLAPPER
(2010)

Raphael Klapper (1925–2010) was an eye doctor. He was from the Bronx, New York. Klapper died at age 85. He had cancer.

Six months after he died, he was on a ballot. He was a candidate for the New York Senate. This happened in 2010. Klapper was 1 of 5 candidates. Klapper got 828 votes. This was 2 percent of the vote.

His family said he had no interest in running for office. People had signed him up. They didn't know he had died. It was a mistake. An election lawyer said, "It's hard to believe that no one knew he was dead."

HOT-BUTTON ISSUE

Hot-button issues refer to tough topics. People have strong emotions. They take sides. To win elections, candidates spend a lot of money. They also spend a lot of time raising money. Money is needed to buy ads. It's needed to travel. It's needed to pay staff. Candidates without money have a harder time. Some think this is unfair. It means only rich people win. It also means rich donors have more power. Most Americans want to limit campaign spending. They want new laws that reduce money in politics. But some Americans think money is part of the process. Candidates need to spread their message. They need their voters to know them. This means they need to pay for media coverage. There is a special group. It's called the Federal Election Commission. They oversee who spends money. They oversee how money is spent. They enforce laws.

CHAPTER EIGHT
MAE POULET
(2012)

Charlotte Laws (born 1960) is an animal rights activist. She was elected to the Greater Valley Glen Council. Valley Glen is a neighborhood in Los Angeles, California.

Laws is more famous for her pet chicken. The chicken is named Mae Poulet. In 2012, Mae became a vice presidential candidate. Satchel is a dog from Tennessee. He was running for president. He chose Mae to be his running mate. Mae and Satchel were a team.

Laws said of Mae, "She has humble beginnings. She can identify with the little person. She's a compassionate chicken." In 2013, Mae was **inducted** into the National Museum of Animals and Society. Induct means to formally admit.

When asked about Mae Poulet, her spokesman said, "We need a new pecking order in America. It's time to elect a chick to the White House."

Chapter Nine
Andrew Basiago
(2016)

Andrew Basiago (born 1961) is a lawyer. He ran for president in 2016. He claimed he would have been the first president to time travel.

Basiago has told many people his story. From ages 7 to 12, he said he was in a secret government program. The program was called Project Pegasus. It researched time travel. It used children in its tests. Children could adapt well when moving through time. Basiago said he went to the Civil War (1861–1865). He said he was in a picture from Abraham Lincoln's reading of the Gettysburg Address. This speech was made in 1863.

Basiago claims the government is hiding the truth. His slogan was "A Time for Truth." Many people don't believe Basiago's claims.

FACT-CHECK

It's important to check facts. Facts must be correct. Here are some fun facts about candidates:

- The University of British Columbia (UBC) is in Canada. It has a student council. In 2004, a fire hydrant was on the student council ballot. Fire hydrants supply water. They help put out fires. The UBC fire hydrant got 22 percent of the votes. It finished 5th of 8 candidates. It ran again in 2005. It did much better. It was 6 votes away from winning. It ran for the 3rd time in 2006. It lost by 48 votes. It finished 3rd.

- Cacareco was a female black rhinoceros. She lived in a zoo in Brazil. People were protesting the 1958 city council elections. They entered Cacareco in the election. Cacareco was rejected. But she still got 100,000 votes. Today, "Cacareco vote" means protest vote in Brazil.

- Michael Moore is a filmmaker. He tried to get a potted tree on the ballot. He wanted the tree to run for Congress. He did this in 2000.

CHAPTER TEN
ZOLTAN ISTVAN
(2016)

Zoltan Istvan (born 1973) is a journalist. He's also a businessman. He's a futurist. Futurists study the future. They predict trends.

Istvan went on a trip to Vietnam. He almost stood on a **land mine**. Land mines are bombs. The tour guide saved his life. Istvan said, "It was time to really dedicate myself to stopping death. Stopping death for me. And stopping death for my loved ones."

He ran for president. He did this in 2016 and 2020. He also ran for California governor. He promised to end death. He traveled across the country. His car was a school bus. The bus was shaped like a coffin.

Istvan thinks technology is powerful. He believes tech can help humans live forever. It can create superhumans.

Zoltan Istvan's political party is called the Transhumanist Party.

DO YOUR PART!

U.S. citizens have 2 special rights. Only U.S. citizens can vote in federal elections. Only U.S. citizens can run for **federal office**. Federal office means a national office. It's different from state and local offices.

U.S. citizens have many other rights. But they also have duties. The most powerful is the duty to vote. Voting is how people choose leaders. It's how people make changes. It's how people promote their ideas. Those elected make the laws. They make policies. They make the rules. They work for voters.

U.S. citizens can vote at age 18. But people are never too young to get involved in democracy.

Many people encourage others to vote.
They are passionate about voting.

Citizens should run for office. Students are too young for public offices. They should start with their schools. Schools have elections. Here are some ideas to be a school leader:

★ Learn about your school's offices. Read about each position. See which one you like best.

★ Write a good speech. State your beliefs. State what you stand for. Be as interesting as you can. Include a slogan.

★ Make posters. Post them all over. Make the posters stand out.

Everyone can do their part. Being a good citizen is hard work. But the work is worth it. Your vote is your voice.

School elections are a good way to learn about leadership.

GLOSSARY

ballot (BA-luht) voting ticket that lists all the election candidates

campaigns (kam-PAYNZ) organized courses of action to achieve a goal such as winning an election

candidates (KAN-duh-dayts) people who want to be elected to certain positions

convict (KAHN-vikt) a person found guilty of a criminal offense

democracy (dih-MAH-kruh-see) a system of government led by voters, often through elected representatives

elect (ih-LEKT) to choose someone to hold public office by voting

extort (ik-STORT) to obtain something by force, threats, or other unfair means

federal office (FEH-druhl AW-fuhs) an elected position in the national government

inducted (in-DUKT-uhd) formally admitted into a position or organization

land mine (LAND MYEN) a bomb placed just below the surface of the ground and designed to explode when stepped on

loopholes (LOOP-holz) unclear sections of laws or policies that allow people to avoid following a rule

precinct captain (PREE-sinkt KAP-tuhn) an elected official who connects political parties and voters and help with the election process

public office (PUH-blik AW-fuhs) government position established by law

represent (reh-prih-ZENT) to speak or act for another person or group

slogan (SLOH-guhn) a short, memorable phrase used in advertising

LEARN MORE

Books

Mahoney, Emily. *Becoming a State Governor*. New York: Gareth Stevens Publishing, 2015.

McPartland, Lisa. *Presidential Campaigns*. New York: PowerKids Press, 2020.

Rebhun, Elliot. *How America Works: Understanding Your Government and How You Can Get Involved*. New York: Scholastic Teaching Resources, 2020.

INDEX

animal candidates, 8–10, 13, 16–17, 22–23, 25

Basiago, Andrew, 24
Boston Curtis (mule), 8–9

Cacareco (rhinoceros), 25
campaign spending, 21
candidates, 4, 6
    animals, 8–10, 13, 16–17, 22–23, 25
    humans, 14–15, 16–17, 20, 24, 26–27
    objects, 11, 12, 25
Clay Henry (goat), 16–17
congressional elections, 13, 20, 25
convicted criminals, 16–17

dead persons, 20

Democratic National Convention (1768), 10
election laws, 6–7, 17, 21, 28

inanimate object candidates, 11, 12, 25
Istvan, Zoltan, 26–27

Judd, Keith Russell, 16

Klapper, Raphael, 20

Mae Poulet (chicken), 22–23
mayoral and city elections
    animals, 8, 16–17, 25
    humans, 14, 16
    objects, 11, 12
mayors, honorary, 13
money in politics, 21

Moore, Michael, 25
Mr. Potato Head, 12

Pigasus (pig), 10
presidential elections, 6–7, 10, 14–15, 16–17, 22–23, 24, 26
Pulvapies (foot powder), 11

school elections, 25, 30–31
Simmons, Kenneth, 8
slogans, 11, 12, 24
Stubbs (cat), 13
Supreme, Vermin Love, 14–15

voting and voting rights, 4, 5, 7, 28–30

Youth International Party (Yippies), 10